W9-ASY-092

Date: 10/6/15

J 639.9 HAL
Halls, Kelly Milner,
Tiger in trouble! : and more
true stories of amazing

TIGER IN TROUBLE!

And More True
Stories of Amazing
Animal Rescues

Published by the National Geographic Society
John M. Fahey, Jr., *Chairman of the Board and Chief Executive Officer*
Timothy T. Kelly, *President*
Declan Moore, *Executive Vice President; President, Publishing and Digital Media*
Melina Gerosa Bellows, *Executive Vice President; Chief Creative Officer, Books, Kids, and Family*

Prepared by the Book Division
Hector Sierra, *Senior Vice President and General Manager*
Nancy Laties Feresten, *Senior Vice President, Editor in Chief, Children's Books*
Jonathan Halling, *Design Director, Books and Children's Publishing*
Jay Sumner, *Director of Photography, Children's Publishing*
Jennifer Emmett, *Editorial Director, Children's Books*
Eva Absher-Schantz, *Managing Art Director, Children's Books*
Carl Mehler, *Director of Maps*
R. Gary Colbert, *Production Director*
Jennifer A. Thornton, *Director of Managing Editorial*

Staff for This Book
Becky Baines and Laura F. Marsh, *Project Editors*
Lori Epstein, *Illustrations Editor*
Eva Absher-Schantz, *Art Director*
YAY! Design, *Designer*
Grace Hill, *Associate Managing Editor*
Joan Gossett, *Production Editor*
Lewis R. Bassford, *Production Manager*
Susan Borke, *Legal and Business Affairs*
Kate Olesin, *Assistant Editor*
Kathryn Robbins, *Design Production Assistant*
Hillary Moloney, *Illustrations Assistant*

Manufacturing and Quality Management
Phillip L. Schlosser, *Senior Vice President*
Chris Brown, *Vice President, NG Book Manufacturing*
George Bounelis, *Vice President, Production Services*
Nicole Elliott, *Manager*
Rachel Faulise, *Manager*
Robert L. Barr, *Manager*

For more information, please call
1-800-NGS LINE (647-5463) or
write to the following address:
National Geographic Society
1145 17th Street N.W.
Washington, D.C. 20036-4688 U.S.A.

Visit us online at nationalgeographic.com/books

For librarians and teachers: ngchildrensbooks.org

More for kids from National Geographic:
kids.nationalgeographic.com

For information about special discounts for bulk purchases, please contact National Geographic Books Special Sales: ngspecsales@ngs.org

For rights or permissions inquiries, please contact National Geographic Books Subsidiary Rights: ngbookrights@ngs.org

Trade paperback ISBN: 978-1-4263-1078-2
Reinforced library edition ISBN:
978-1-4263-1079-9

Printed in China
12/RRDS/1

Table of CONTENTS

Nitro, a 600-pound tiger, is cared for by Carolina Tiger Rescue.

NITRO: TIGER IN TROUBLE

Nitro's Kansas home was a tiny cage in a junkyard.

en-year-old Nitro paced in his cage. It was the evening of February 21, 2009. The sun was setting quickly. Nitro's owner, Jeffrey Harsh, was late with the tiger's dinner.

Hungry big cats get restless, but Nitro couldn't pace far. His chain-link cage was only 20 feet wide and 30 feet long—one-third the size of a school gym. Nitro was eight feet long. He could only take a few steps. Then he had to turn and walk the other way. Back and forth. Back and forth.

He stepped over bones in the dust. They were left over from earlier meals. He brushed against Apache, the other tiger in his cage. His empty belly grumbled. He growled and roared.

Nitro and Apache were not alone. There were three female lions in other cages nearby. All of these big cats were living at the Prairie Cat Animal Refuge near Oakley, Kansas—and they were all hungry.

A man wandered to the main gate. The cats' eyes locked on him. He opened the gate and slowly came inside.

The man passed piles of junk.

He looked into each animal's cage. Nitro listened, while the other cats studied the stranger.

Then the man walked toward a lioness. He slipped his hand inside the metal bars of her gate.

It was a very bad choice.

To the hungry lion, his arm looked like dinner. Her instinct told her to catch her meal, and she listened. She bit down on the stranger's arm. He screamed and screamed.

Just then Jeffrey drove up with a truck full of meat. He could tell right away things were not right. The entry gate was unlocked and open. Screams were coming from the big cats' cages. Jeffrey jumped out of his truck and ran toward the sound.

Jeffrey saw the stranger. He ran past

Nitro, toward the lion cage. Jeffrey grabbed the man and tried to pull him free. But he wasn't as strong as the lion, and she would not let go. He never hit the animals, but he didn't know what else to do. The man was in serious danger.

Jeffrey picked up a metal pipe and swung at the lioness. At last, she opened her jaws, and the frightened man fell back. Jeffrey rushed the stranger to the hospital. As he drove, he called the police on his cell phone.

Nitro would have to wait a little longer for his dinner. His owner was under arrest. He had not protected the stranger from the dangerous big cats.

Until that night, Jeffrey Harsh had broken no laws. Almost half of the states in the U.S. have passed laws to make it illegal to own wild animals like Nitro. Thirteen other states have some rules that say who can keep them and who cannot. The rest of the states have almost no laws at all. There, almost anyone can buy a wild animal.

Kansas is one of the 13 states with some rules. But the rules are not strong enough, said Sheriff Rod Taylor, the officer who arrested Jeffrey. Owners do not even need to take a class to learn how to care for a wild animal. If people like Jeffrey Harsh follow a few rules, they can buy big cats and raise them. And terrible things can happen.

Jeffrey didn't see it that way. He didn't think his big cats would hurt anyone.

He thought since his animals were raised in captivity, or in cages, they would not act like wild animals.

"They were born in captivity," he said on his website, "and bottle fed, so they think they are human. They are as gentle and sweet as a house cat." He was wrong.

The judge gave Jeffrey a choice. He could pay fines and spend months in jail, or he could give the big cats to people who knew how to take care of them. Jeffrey decided to give his pets away. The lionesses were headed to the Detroit Zoo. But this zoo didn't need any tigers. No zoo did.

Did You Know?

Every tiger has stripes, but not all stripes are alike. In fact, none of them are. No two tigers have exactly the same pattern.

So You Think You Want a Baby Tiger?

Keeping a baby tiger as a pet might seem like a great idea. At first, they weigh only a few pounds. And they don't have teeth. They are cute and harmless.

But as they grow bigger and stronger, tigers play rough. They can hurt their owners. It is better to visit a tiger in a zoo or animal rescue. They don't belong in people's homes.

So where would Nitro and Apache go?

Sheriff Taylor called animal rescue experts for help. They told him about Carolina Tiger Rescue in North Carolina. Would they agree to take Nitro and Apache? That was the big question.

Kathryn Bertok works at Carolina Tiger Rescue. She takes care of the animals that live there.

"We won't take an animal unless we can take them for the rest of their lives," Kathryn explained. That's because moving a tiger is hard. It is hard for the tiger. It is also hard for the people moving it.

Tigers that are cared for by humans can live to be 20 years old. Nitro and Apache were 10 years old. Tiger Rescue would have to pay the cost of feeding and caring for two tigers for ten more years. Could they afford it?

There was another important question: How much space would Nitro and Apache need? Big cats get sad in small spaces. They pace in a figure-eight pattern. They pant and grumble. They even suck their tails, like a baby human sucks its thumb.

The tiny cage in Kansas was far too small for two full-grown cats. A new home for Nitro and Apache would need to be bigger. Much bigger. It would take a space 37 times as big as their Kansas cage to keep them happy.

Experts at Carolina Tiger Rescue thought long and hard.

At last, they answered yes.

The experts at Carolina Tiger Rescue know how to care for and move big cats.

To the RESCUE

Moving Nitro and Apache from Kansas to North Carolina would be a tiger-size challenge. Even so, Kathryn was sure she could do it.

Kathryn loaded the Rescue's truck. She put in two large crates—one for Nitro and one for Apache. She also took along tools and fence cutters. The tiger cubs had grown large in their little chain-link cage.

They were now too big to get in and out through the door. Kathryn might have to cut the cage apart.

On April 12, 2009, Kathryn arrived in Oakley, Kansas. She had been driving for 26 hours. She checked into a hotel and got ready for a good night's sleep. Saving two tigers would not be easy. Kathryn would need all her strength and energy.

Kathryn, Sheriff Taylor, and an animal doctor called a veterinarian (vet) met at the front gate of the Prairie Cat Animal Refuge. Nitro was awake. He heard new voices and smelled unfamiliar scents. The strangers made him feel uneasy. He paced and softly grumbled.

Kathryn could tell that the tigers were calm. But they did not seem to trust her.

"Animals can sense when something big is about to happen," she said.

It was time for Nitro and Apache to take a nap. The vet had a special dart gun to shoot medicine into the tigers. If the darts hit just right, Nitro and Apache would be fast asleep in no time. They would sleep while the team moved them. Then they would wake up safe and sound inside their travel crates. The vet knew just the right amount of medicine to use.

POP. POP. The vet pulled the trigger, and the darts hit their targets.

Nitro hissed quietly when the dart hit his shoulder. His ears fell flat against his head. He was afraid. Then he felt the medicine start to work. He settled down. His stomach was flat on the dusty earth.

His breathing slowed down. He fell into a deep and peaceful sleep.

Quickly, Kathryn cut a large hole in the chain-link fence. She and the others climbed through the hole into the cage. Gently, they loaded Nitro into a large travel crate. It looked like a crate for a very large dog.

Nitro woke a short time later. He was safely loaded into the Carolina Tiger Rescue truck. Kathryn drove east, out of Kansas. Nitro was slightly confused, but not afraid.

"It depends on the animal," Kathryn said. "But these guys were fine. When you get on the road, they tend to settle down, like kids. The movement of the truck relaxes them."

Every two hours, Nitro saw his new caretakers. They stopped to check on him and give him food or water. Twenty-six hours later, Nitro was at the rescue. But it would still be another month before he could move into his forever home.

The concrete cells where Nitro and Apache first stayed weren't very comfortable. The hard surface felt strange against Nitro's paws. But the cells were clean and safe.

The people at the rescue needed to keep Nitro and Apache separated. They could not be near the other cats for 30 days. During that time, the tigers would get a full medical checkup by the veterinarians.

If they had any diseases, the vets could find out before they passed it on to other tigers. They would also check Nitro and Apache for injuries and give them medicine if they needed it. Only after that could the tigers be around other animals.

The veterinarian put Nitro to sleep again. This time, it was a much deeper sleep because the vet had a lot to do. Nitro needed his teeth cleaned. He had to get shots. And he needed to have a tiny microchip placed just under his skin. Then he could be tracked and returned to Carolina Tiger Rescue if he was ever lost or stolen.

How Much Does a Captive Tiger Eat?

Some wild tigers can eat 40 pounds of meat each day. Others can gobble down as much as 70 pounds.

Tigers in the wild are more active than tigers in captivity. They hunt for miles. Wild tigers also eat a lot when they can because weeks can pass between meals.

At Carolina Tiger Rescue, the diet is different. Tigers eat smaller meals—15 to 20 pounds of meat. Also, they eat five days a week. Nitro eats whole chickens, beef, goats, and deer.

"It's not pretty," Kathryn said. "But it's important to their health."

When most big cats wake up, they are a little sleepy, but otherwise healthy. Nitro was not most big cats.

As he woke, Nitro began to moan and pant. He could hardly stand, and he was confused. Kathryn had seen it before—Nitro was suffering from hyperthermia (sounds like hi-per-THUR-mee-uh). That meant he could not control his body temperature. His fever was rising quickly. If the staff didn't act fast to cool him, he might not survive.

Kathryn brought out water hoses. Each animal caretaker took turns bathing Nitro's body with cool water. They needed to keep his fever down. "His paws went bright pink when he was in trouble," she said. "Keeping him cool really helped."

After two days, Nitro was finally getting better. He was hungry. He even started to walk around his cage. But Kathryn noticed something strange.

Three of the four walls of the cage were made of concrete. The fourth wall was made of chain link. Most animals faced the chain-link wall. They like to watch what is going on outside of their cage. Nitro did not.

"He would sit and stare at the concrete walls," Kathryn said. "And when he did turn toward our voices, he would follow the sound of our voices. But not our movements."

Kathryn knew this meant one thing: Nitro was blind.

Caretakers at the Tiger Rescue thought of ways to help blind Nitro find his way around his cage.

Now that he was healthy, Nitro was ready for his new cage. But he couldn't see it. His owner in Kansas had never noticed Nitro was blind. That cage had been so small, Nitro had been able to memorize every inch. So, he may not have seemed blind.

Why was Nitro blind? That's hard to tell.

Kathryn ruled out a brain injury.

And there were no scars around Nitro's eyes that might mean he had an injury. "We just don't know what caused his condition," Kathryn said.

Here's what they did know. The caretakers at the Rescue had a big challenge ahead of them. They had to help a blind tiger find his way, without the use of his eyes.

Nitro walked through his big new home. He reached out with huge six-inch paws. He was trying to feel what was ahead of him. He did not know where things were around him. Not a twig, not a path, not a feeding dish.

He was a little afraid. He could never tell when he was getting close to running into the fence.

"He was roughing up his nose, because he would walk right up to the fence and hit it," Kathryn said. "We kept thinking, 'you have to slow down.'" But how do you teach a blind tiger how to find a fence he cannot see?

"We decided to start marking the fence with peppermint," Kathryn explained. "He would know when he smelled it, he should slow down. The peppermint marked the borders of his space."

Once he learned where his fences were, the people at the Rescue put down sand pathways. The sand pathways led to Nitro's food, water, and his cozy den.

When Nitro felt sand under his paws, he knew he would end up in one of those areas. When Nitro felt leaves, dirt, and twigs, he knew he was not heading in the right direction.

In time, Nitro learned where every bump, every tree, and every food box was in his new cage. When he did, the sand and the peppermint could be put away. Nitro was finally home.

Caretakers noticed a big change in Nitro. He mastered his space. He couldn't see people. But he knew where they were, even if they stood perfectly still.

He chuffled in their direction to get them to answer. He wanted to hear if he knew their voices. He wanted to know who they were.

Did You Know?

What's a chuffle? It's the sound a tiger makes when it sees or smells a friend. It sounds like a purr with a tiny cough.

Nitro, the blind tiger, has become a Rescue favorite. Volunteers guide people through Carolina Tiger Rescue once a week. They never miss a stop at Nitro's cage. They tell his story and give him little treats (scraps of chicken or beef). Nitro never disappoints.

"He has a great attitude," Kathryn says. "Things haven't been easy for him. But he still comes up to the fence happily chuffling."

Caretakers agree. Nitro is a trusting tiger. He never seems cranky or mad. Even so, he was and still is a tough, wild tiger. He still has his kill instincts.

In many ways, Nitro acts like a pet cat. He takes catnaps. He scratches his claws on trees, like a house cat would use a scratching post. He rolls in the dirt. He licks his fur to groom himself. He likes to play by crouching and then pouncing.

Still, Nitro's size and weight would make those playful swats and scratches deadly. If a house cat gets scared and claws your hand, you need a bandage. If a tiger gets scared and uses its claws, you could get a cut that needs stitches. Or something worse.

The tiger isn't "turning mean." It's showing behavior that keeps it alive in the wild.

In the wild, tigers are solitary animals, which means they live alone. They need to protect themselves and find food. Their keen eyes notice even the smallest movements. They pounce with their powerful legs. Tigers hold the animals they catch tightly, so they can't get away. They kill the animals quickly. Then they defend the food they catch with sharp claws, so other tigers won't steal it.

Tigers at zoos or rescues do not need to use the rough behavior tigers use in the wild. Tigers in captivity don't need to find their own food. And they won't be attacked by other animals.

But in captivity or in the wild, tigers have the same kill instincts.

Creating more laws to help big cats would stop some unhappy endings for tigers like Nitro. If every state makes owning tigers against the law, only zoos and special programs could raise them.

Fewer animals would be mistreated or killed.

Nitro, the tiger in trouble, will be safe from now on. He spends his days wandering around his huge cage. He naps in his den, and he trots toward people who visit him. He roars at the other cats in the rescue, and they answer him. Nitro is happy, and he is loved.

The people at Carolina Tiger Rescue will take care of him for the rest of his life. Even Nitro can "see" how great that ending turned out to be.

Kids Can Help

Here are some ideas to help big cats like Nitro:

- Organize a penny drive: Set up jars or cans at school. Ask people to donate their pennies. Send the money to a big cat rescue group.

- Sponsor a big cat: Families or classrooms can sponsor a big cat at Carolina Tiger Rescue. This helps pay for its care.

- Learn about National Geographic's Big Cat Initiative at animals.national geographic.com/animals/big-cats/about.

- Support countries that protect tigers and their habitats by visiting there.

Learn more about Carolina Tiger Rescue at www.carolinatigerrescue.org.

Bats at rest fold their delicate wings close to their bodies.

ETHEREAL: AN ALBINO BAT BABY

There are about 1,000 species of bats in the world. Ethereal is a Mexican free-tailed bat.

LOST And FOUND

The tiny bat was hungry. She had to go hunting for something to eat. But she knew she was taking a chance.

She soared into the Texas air. She needed to catch enough insects to stay alive. She liked all kinds of insects. There were moths, dragonflies, beetles, and many others. But other animals were also hunting. She needed to be careful.

Her pink wings spread. They lifted her tiny body high into the night sky.

She was a Mexican free-tailed bat. This kind of bat is one of the fastest animals in the world. She had no trouble darting and weaving.

She sent out sound waves. Each one bounced back to tell her what was ahead. They also told her where she might find her next meal. She was using echolocation (sounds like eck-oh-low-KAY-shun).

Sometimes, the sound waves told her she was near something too big to eat. It might be a tree branch or a big animal. Sometimes, the sound waves said she was near something too small to be a tasty bug. Sometimes, the waves were just right. Then she knew she was close to something yummy and just her size.

The little bat found a flying June bug, and she dived toward the juicy snack. Moonlight shone on her fur. She was easy to see against the pitch-black sky.

She zipped and zoomed toward her meal. But she was not the only one looking for dinner.

Just then a barn owl swooped out of the darkness. He flew full speed toward the tiny bat. His sharp claws opened as he moved in toward her small body.

The bat used every trick she knew to escape. Hunting would have to wait. She changed direction. She flew toward an old house below her.

Heart pounding, she sailed through the open window. She landed on the wooden rafters and tried to catch her breath.

Blending in was just too hard, no matter how she tried. The tiny bat had albinism (sounds like AL-been-iz-um), which made her fur white.

With no brown color, the little white bat looked like a tiny angel. She moved, inch by inch, across the beams. She was tired and weak. And now she would have another night without food. The poor bat was starving.

But she was in luck. It would be her last hungry night. The old house she flew into was owned by Bat World Sanctuary.

Bat World Sanctuary rescues and protects bats. The staff also teach people about bats. The starving little bat had found just the right place to rest.

What Is Albinism?

Ethereal has albinism. This means that her body does not make pigment. Pigment adds color to skin, hair, and eyes. It also protects skin from the sun.

What causes albinism? It's an accident of nature. It doesn't happen very often. Most parents of albino babies are not albinos themselves. They usually have typical coloring.

Most animals with albinism don't see very well. But echolocation helped the little white bat hunt without using her eyes.

Many thousands of Mexican free-tailed bats were living in the old home. They slept during the day. They huddled together to keep warm. As many as 500 baby bats or 200 adult bats dangled from each square foot of the ceiling. The places where they hung are called roosts. At night, they flew out to hunt for insects.

The people at Bat World were studying the huge group of bats living there. Bats are the only flying mammals on Earth. Mammals have fur and give birth to their young. Mammal babies also drink their mother's milk. Unlike birds, baby bats drink milk until they are old enough to hunt for bugs on their own.

Staff members would leave their main office every few days to check for wounded bats. This is especially important in June and July, when new bat pups are born.

Owls and hawks eat young Mexican free-tailed bats. Snakes, raccoons, and house cats do, too. If young bats fall from their high roosts, the mother bats do not rescue them. People at Bat World rescue them instead.

Amanda Lollar is the director of Bat World. She is the person who discovered the little white bat the next day. "When we saw her 15 feet above us, she stood out like a spotlight," Amanda said.

Usually, Amanda and her team take rescued bats to their main office. They don't plan to keep them forever. They hope to make them healthy. Then they release them into the Texas sky.

But this bat was different.

The bat was about eight weeks old. She had just stopped drinking her mother's milk. She was trying to hunt on her own. "But she hadn't been getting enough to eat," Amanda said. The tiny bat couldn't hunt enough to keep herself fed. She was so often hunted herself.

She had no dark color to blend into the dark night sky. The bat would never be able to live in the wild. Amanda decided to give her a new home. She would live at Bat World forever.

Volunteers from Bat World carefully caught the tiny white mammal. They gently placed her in a box. Then they drove her to their indoor sanctuary. There she got a complete checkup and a tasty dinner. Plus, she got a brand-new name—Ethereal (sounds like uh-THEE-ree-ul).

Why the name Ethereal? It means delicate or heavenly. "She was just so beautiful," Amanda said. "So otherworldly—like a little fairy. The name seemed to fit."

Ethereal loves mealtime! Even the small feeding syringe looks big next to the tiny bat.

FOOD and Friendship

ike magic, Ethereal made friends with Amanda. "Bats are very smart," she said. "They may be as smart as dolphins. Ethereal knew we wanted to help her. She got used to us right away. She is a sweet, sweet little bat. Ethereal is shy with new people, but most bats are."

Close friendship is healthy for a bat. But being friends with just one person can be dangerous, too. That person might have to go away. A new person might come instead.

"If we don't prepare the bats for the change, they might stop eating," Amanda explained.

Food made the friendship between Amanda and Ethereal stronger. Like the bat's mother, Amanda was taking care of the little bat, and Ethereal knew it.

In the wild, Mexican free-tailed bats eat insects. Those insects eat flowers and fruits and vegetables. So, eating those bugs is a little like eating fruits and vegetables, too. The vitamins in those bugs make them good meals for bats.

Ethereal and the other bats at Bat World stay inside in huge rooms called flying cages. The bats can fly and play, chat and sleep, but they don't hunt for wild insects. Wild bugs aren't allowed in the flying cages because some could make the bats sick. So, Amanda makes healthy food for them.

"Bats that never really ate in the wild are given a soft food diet," Amanda said. "This includes mealworm guts."

The mealworms are full of vitamins and protein. They give bats lots of energy to swoop and soar. The Bat World workers use 200,000 mealworms every month to feed the bats.

Amanda makes sure every bat gets plenty to eat—just enough to make them healthy. But Ethereal has a favorite.

"She loves peaches," Amanda said.

"She's excited when peaches are in the mix." She slurps up the sticky stuff especially fast when her favorite food is served.

Did You Know?

A baby Mexican free-tailed bat weighs about as much as a stick of gum.

Some bats are fed food in feeding dishes. The dishes are piled high with mealworms and ripe fruits like berries and peaches. The bats gather at the dishes to eat.

Other bats like Ethereal are fed by hand. Volunteers measure vitamins, worm guts, fruit, and vegetables. Then they mash them up with a blender. Amanda fills a syringe (sounds like ser-INGE) with the tasty goo. It's dinner time!

One at a time, Amanda gathers each

bat into her left hand. She squeezes very carefully to hold it firmly. The bat puts its tiny, wrinkled lips on the syringe to eat.

With her right hand, Amanda slowly squirts the food into the bat's hungry mouth. The bat gobbles up the mixture. Amanda is very careful not to go too quickly. Too much food at one time could choke the bat. Also, she doesn't want to get food in the bat's tiny nose. When she's done, Amanda wipes each dirty little face.

It takes time to feed each bat by hand. But hand-feeding helps the bats learn to trust the caretakers.

Do the little bats like being hand fed? Amanda thinks so.

"At feeding times, we slip the bats into carriers. We call them 'bat huts,'" Amanda said. They move the bat huts filled with bats to the feeding room. If Amanda places the bat huts in the cages early, something amazing happens.

"They will load themselves into the bat huts," Amanda said. They know bat-hut time means mealtime!

Ethereal was not fed with the other bats at first. She was not allowed near any other animals. She was kept apart until Amanda knew she was healthy. If Ethereal were sick, she could make other bats sick, too.

Luckily, Ethereal was fine. The tiny bat's new life could begin. She had already started to eat better. She was getting her strength back.

More About Mexican Free-tailed Bats

In June, Mexican free-tailed bat mothers have tiny babies called pups. Each mother usually has one baby.

The mammal pup drinks its mother's milk. After it eats, the pup sleeps away from its mother. Hundreds of pups sleep together in one small space. Then the mothers leave to hunt for bugs.

How do mothers find their babies when they return? A mother can tell her pup by its voice and its familiar smell.

The next step was moving Ethereal to her new home. How bats live depends on what kind of bat they are.

"Tree bats live alone," Amanda said. "They mind their own business. Crevice bats are social. They get sad when they are alone."

"Ethereal is a crevice bat," Amanda said. "She needs friends."

Ethereal was placed in a cage with many other bats of her own kind. The other bats took a little getting used to.

So, Amanda gave Ethereal a safe place of her own—a basket on the floor of the huge cage. From the basket, she could watch the other bats. She could get out of the nest if she wanted to make new friends. She could stay in if she was feeling shy.

Amanda didn't rush Ethereal. She let her make friends when she was ready, so she wouldn't be afraid.

Soon Ethereal got used to the other bats. She spent more and more time playing with them. She chattered in little squeaks and clicks and hisses, and flew with them. She was learning more about them. She was becoming part of the colony.

Amanda feeds Ethereal in her bat hut. The bat pokes her head out to ask for more dinner.

Chapter 3

Life in a NEW HOME

Ethereal was settling in. It was time to explore her new world. Then she would really feel at home.

Ethereal soared through the giant cage. She darted from corner to corner. She landed on dozens of roosts. She hung upside down. She could go anywhere. There were no hungry meat eaters in sight.

The other bats felt the same.

There were 150 bats in the colony. They dangled from the ceiling beside her. She fit right in. The other bats didn't seem to notice she wasn't the same color they were.

"In some species, other animals won't go near one that's different," Amanda said. "But Ethereal was accepted by the normal bats at Bat World."

Ethereal was getting to know the other bats. Every bat has its own personality and voice. "I study them," Amanda said, "And I've found at least 25 different sounds." That's like knowing 25 special bat words.

Amanda doesn't know what the bats are saying. But she does think they're talking with each other. She believes the bats put sounds together to have conversations. She thinks they may even make bat sentences. "I believe they are that smart," she said.

Ethereal settled right into the chatter. She even picked a ceiling roost of her very own.

"Ethereal lands in one spot almost every time," said Amanda. "She knows she is at home."

Making good friends was next on Ethereal's list. Which bats would be her pals? It took a few weeks to decide. She finally settled on a small group of female bats. She had found best friends of her very own.

How can you tell when bats are best friends? "They snuggle," Amanda said. "They chitter and peep and stay close together."

Ethereal chitters with three of the other girl bats most of the time. She likes Batzilla, Barbie, and Princess Ugly Toe.

The four girls get along great. But they do have little fights now and then. They chirp and chitter and fuss. Sometimes, they even hiss.

"It's like a soap opera," Amanda said with a laugh. But they really hang out. They actually dangle together, side by side.

Someday, Ethereal may have a mate. She may even have a pup of her own. "It's possible," said Amanda. "She's healthy. The boys treat her like all the other girls. They don't mind that she's an albino.

But for now, she doesn't seem interested. For now, she's happy as one of the girls."

That's okay, because Ethereal has an important job to do. She is teaching scientists about albino bats.

"We don't know much about albinism in bats," said Amanda. Studying Ethereal will help Bat World and other scientists understand albino bats a little better. Amanda will share all the facts she discovers.

Ethereal has another job to do. She teaches people who aren't scientists all about bats.

Ethereal goes to schools and community events. She is on the Bat World website. Many people get to meet her and learn more about her. They find out about all of the interesting things bats do—and what they don't do.

Some people think bats like to tangle themselves in human hair. But that's not true. Some people think all bats drink blood, but only South American vampire bats do. And vampire bats rarely try to drink human blood.

Other bat species do not drink blood at all. They eat fruit and insects—lots of insects. That is why farmers love bats. Insects damage the food farmers grow. So, when bats eat insects, they help keep farmers' crops safe. Ethereal can help Amanda and Bat World teach people the truth about bats.

Only five other bats at Bat World are friendly enough to do this work. Amanda said she chose Ethereal because she is so sweet. "I would never take a bat with me if it wasn't calm with people," she said. "It would be far too scary for the bat."

Bats also are sensitive. "You know how a cat can tell when someone doesn't like it?" Amanda said. "Bats are the same. If they sense you're trying to help them, they're friendly. If they think you don't really like bats, they act scared of you."

Amanda wants people to meet a sweet bat like Ethereal. Then they will realize what great animals bats are. Amanda has worked with bats for 20 years. She wants to stop other people from being scared of them. She hopes they will start seeing bats as friends.

Ethereal has a long life ahead of her.

A Mexican free-tailed bat can live 15 years in captivity.

"We had one orphan, named Andrea, who lived to be 19 years old," said Amanda. Ethereal might not live quite that long. But every day she is alive is a reason to be happy.

"She's such a little angel," Amanda said. "I hope she'll be happy and safe for a long, long time."

How Kids Can Help

It's never a good idea to keep a bat as a pet. But you can still help a flying mammal like Ethereal. Here's how:

You or your class can adopt a bat. Your donation provides food, medicine, and bat toys for a Bat World Sanctuary bat. You'll get a certificate, a photo, and regular updates on your bat.

To adopt a bat, visit Bat World Sanctuary at www.batworld.org/ adopt-a-bat-now.

If bats live where you live, you could build an outdoor bat house. The Bat Conservation International website tells you how. Visit www.batcon.org.

Suzie, Bob, and Caleb play well together at the Primate Rescue Center.

SUZIE, BOB, & CALEB: The Three Monkeyteers

Bob likes to wrestle and play. Vervet monkeys are good jumpers and climbers.

Chapter 1

ESCAPE
From Tiny Cages

Could an old Olive baboon and two baby Vervet monkeys make a real family? Maybe not in the wild. But for Suzie, Bob, and Caleb, the weird mix worked. They found each other after tough times alone.

SUZIE

Suzie was very small when she was adopted more than 25 years ago. She weighed less than three pounds. She is an Olive baboon. She had thick black fur and a sweet pink face. Suzie was so cute. People smiled and laughed when they saw her.

The people who bought her didn't break the law. Keeping monkeys was allowed in their Kentucky neighborhood. But they probably didn't know how hard it was for the baboon.

"Babies are pulled from their mothers too soon," said Eileen Dunnington, an expert caretaker at the Primate Rescue Center. "This stops the mother-baby bonding. It is very hurtful to both the mother and baby."

Suzie's owners didn't think about that when they bought her. They thought of how much they would love her. They promised to care for Suzie forever.

Keeping the promise was easy when Suzie was little. Everything was easy when she was small. Her cage in the basement seemed so big. She was hardly ever in her cage because her owners wanted to play with her all the time. Owning a baby Olive baboon was fun.

Then Suzie started to grow.

Her black coat disappeared. The thick olive coat she was named for took its place. She gained weight quickly. In no time, she weighed 32 pounds.

She wasn't a tiny baby anymore. She was more than three feet long. Her cage seemed a whole lot smaller.

Once she wasn't a cute little baby, Suzie

got easier to ignore. Most of the time, Suzie was alone.

Being alone is hard for an Olive baboon. Monkeys like Suzie normally live in Africa, where it is loud and lively with wildlife. Baboon troops have 20 to 100 noisy members. They scamper together across the savannah.

Female troop leaders keep watch over dozens of Olive baboons of all ages. They hunt. They play. They groom one another. They even sleep together.

Suzie slept and ate and daydreamed all by herself.

Food was also a problem for Suzie. In nature, she would have been an omnivore (sounds like OM-nee-vore). That means she would have gobbled up whatever food she could find. Her troop would have wandered for miles. They would have eaten grasses, roots, fruits, and insects. She might have even eaten birds or injured animals, if she was hungry enough.

Suzie's human family didn't have African fruits or vegetables. They didn't have insects or antelope, either. They fed her human food that wasn't healthy for a growing monkey.

Suzie grew fat because she had no way to exercise. She mostly stayed in her cage. She couldn't even stretch her restless, long legs.

Year after year, Suzie got sicker. And she became scared.

When Suzie turned 25 years old, her owners asked for help. They called the Primate Rescue Center in Nicholasville, Kentucky.

BOB

When Bob was born, he was an average little Vervet monkey. He was living with a private breeder.

The breeder raised baby monkeys for money. He sold them to strangers as pets. For some reason, no one wanted to buy Bob.

Bob was cute. He was only a few weeks old. He still had his light-colored baby face and blackish-colored fur. He weighed less than two pounds. He certainly had a lot of energy—too much energy maybe.

Bob got into everything when he was out of his cage. He climbed up curtains. He knocked things over. He didn't have sharp teeth yet. But crazy little Bob was quite a handful.

Weeks passed. The breeder needed Bob's cage for a new baby. So, the breeder's friend agreed to become Bob's foster mother. She took him home with her.

In the wilds of Africa, Bob would have stayed with his mother for four months. He would have gotten the nutrition he needed from her rich milk.

His mother would have taught him how to be a smart Vervet monkey. She would have cared for him for a year, while he learned to hunt. Then his mother would have stopped looking out for him.

Monkey Mothers and Babies

A primate mother bonds with her infant right after it is born. The mother knows her baby's smell. She knows how it looks and how it sounds.

Monkey babies are helpless when they are born. They would die if their mothers didn't care for them so well. The mother's instinct is very strong. If a mother loses her newborn, she may even adopt another mother's baby.

A mother monkey even kisses her baby. She will gently touch her mouth to her little monkey's lips.

Hundreds of other female monkeys would have cuddled him. They would have cared for him, a lot like his mother had done.

In Africa, Bob would have been busy. He would have played, hunted, and groomed himself all day. He would have "talked" to other monkeys. He would never have been lonely. He would have had many friends around.

Bob's new foster mom knew all that. She worried about Bob.

"She was aware of the problem, so she reached out to us," Eileen said. "She wanted to give him the best life possible." So, Bob's foster mom made a decision. The best life outside of Africa would be at the Primate Rescue Center.

CALEB

Like Bob, Caleb was a lively Vervet monkey. Only when he left the breeder who had raised him, he had no trouble finding a home. A man bought him. He kept Caleb in a cage when they weren't playing together.

Then Caleb's owner took a new job. He had to travel a lot. So, he hired a kind babysitter for Caleb.

Again and again, she took Caleb to her house when his owner was away. Soon she grew impatient. She would care for Caleb for weeks at a time. Then she would pack Caleb up and take him back home.

Bouncing from home to home was making Caleb afraid and shy. His babysitter worried. She asked Caleb's owner to let him live with her forever. He agreed.

The babysitter called the Kentucky Department of Fish and Wildlife. She wanted tips on keeping a Vervet monkey baby happy and healthy.

Instead, she found out that keeping Caleb was against the law in her town. Soon Caleb too was on his way to the Primate Rescue Center.

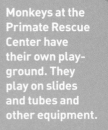

Monkeys at the Primate Rescue Center have their own playground. They play on slides and tubes and other equipment.

Chapter 2

The Healing BEGINS

Suzie, Bob, and Caleb had found their way to safety. But they had not yet found each other. Caretakers at the rescue center had to get to know the monkeys first. Then they could help them feel truly at home.

It isn't good for a monkey to leave its mother too early. It makes it hard for the monkey to trust people or even other monkeys.

Suzie, Bob, and Caleb had all been taken from their mothers too soon. They would need time and help to heal.

At the Primate Rescue Center, the staff works hard to make the transition as easy as possible. "All primates are scared of strangers. Sometimes they seem mean. Suzie, Bob, and Caleb were shy and scared, but not mean," Eileen said.

Suzie, Bob, and Caleb each had their own cage at first. They were in a special building away from other primates. This is where they would spend their first few weeks at the rescue center. The building was calm and quiet. It was also filled with natural light. This helped comfort them a little.

It was the first sunlight Suzie had seen

for years. It helped her relax a little right away. The warm and quiet cage was just right, too.

The veterinarian at the rescue center gave each monkey a checkup. She put them to sleep, just for a little while. Then she looked each monkey over.

The vet took careful measurements of each monkey. She wanted to know how much they weighed and how long they were. This information helps the vet to help the monkeys.

If a monkey gains weight, it usually means it is happy. The monkey is doing well in its new home. If a monkey loses weight, the monkey may not be happy. Then the caretakers know the monkey may need more toys or more time with its caretakers. They watch closely to make sure each monkey is comfortable at the Primate Rescue Center.

The vet also took some blood from each monkey to test for diseases. Some diseases are caused by germs. Germs can hop from one animal or person to another. One blood test showed if the animal has disease germs. Other tests showed diseases not caused by germs.

It turned out Suzie had diabetes (sounds like die-uh-BEE-tees). Diabetes is not caused by germs.

If you have diabetes, your body can't use sugar in the right way. You are often thirsty. You don't have much energy. And you have to go to the bathroom more than an animal without diabetes.

Primate Toys

What kind of presents would keep a monkey happy?

Toys. Monkeys in zoos or rescues need fun toys to keep them active. You might think finding toys for monkeys would be hard, but the Internet makes it easy. Websites sell balls, blankets, swings, and tubes.

Primate toys are extra tough. They come in different sizes for different kinds of monkeys. Best of all, sometimes they come in different flavors. There are even monkey toys that taste like bacon.

Suzie couldn't spread her diabetes to other animals. But it made her feel terrible. She got diabetes from eating unhealthy food all her life. She would need a calm place to live. She would need a special diet and lots of water. She would need to take medicine for the rest of her life.

"Suzie was also very weak. She had not had room to exercise," Eileen said. "But she was so calm and nice. We knew she would adjust. She even took her medicine without a fuss."

Even better, Suzie loved her new meal plan. She ate lots of vegetables. She was on her way to a fit, new life.

Bob and Caleb weren't old enough to have such serious problems. They were each less than a year old when they were rescued. So, they got used to their new home faster than Suzie did.

"We gave them blankets and stuffed animals, so they had something to cling to," Eileen said. "That's a natural behavior for a young primate."

Bob got a healthy report right away. Little Caleb did not.

Caleb had a disease called worms. He had to take a special medicine to make the worms go away. The Rescue caregivers had to be very careful working with him. Otherwise, they could catch worms, too. Being sick helped Caleb because he got lots of one-on-one attention. It was just what he needed. Caleb began to feel better.

"All three of the monkeys were able to bond with the staff," said Eileen. "Soon they came out of their shells. They started to show their true personalities."

Suzie was shy, but kind and gentle. She loved to spend time with the Rescue caretakers. She loved to groom them. She would take her small monkey fingers and comb through the caretakers' hair to search for insects. If she found one, she'd remove it. She also loved to take bits of food from their hands.

Caleb was sweet, but shy and unsure. He would cling to his stuffed animals and soft blankets. He cuddled with them, rocking back and forth, back and forth. It was a sign he missed his mother.

Even so, he loved to play, once he got a little braver.

Bob was a lively, active little monkey. He had so much energy that he drove some of the other monkeys crazy. Bob would climb on them. He would wrestle them. He would nip and chatter and nudge them. He was trying to get them to play.

The monkeys were now getting the medical care they needed. They were getting to know their human caregivers. They were settling into the Primate Rescue Center. But something was missing.

It was time for each of the rescued monkeys to make friends.

Suzie the Olive baboon watches over Bob and Caleb. In the wild, female troop leaders would look out for young monkeys.

Chapter 3

A NEW Kind of FAMILY

Suzie, Bob, and Caleb didn't know it yet. But it was time for them to become friends with other monkeys.

"Some primates are introduced to a group or another monkey and everyone gets along fine," said Eileen. Finding those monkeys a rescue family is easy.

With others, it doesn't go so well. Making the right friendship

match is a little harder with them.

Monkeys get along with their own kind in the wild. Monkeys raised by humans are different.

They haven't learned the things that help monkeys bond with each other. They haven't had to work together to find food. They haven't learned to groom each other. They haven't learned to trust each other. So, making friends can be hard.

Monkeys raised by humans are sometimes very scared when they meet other monkeys. They might act mean because they don't trust other animals yet.

The Primate Rescue Center keeps these monkeys separate from the other monkeys. They give them toys and activities. The toys, called enrichments, keep the monkeys happy and eager to learn. Often, they can see other monkeys in nearby cages. But they know those monkeys can't get too close.

The caretakers hope that these monkeys will calm down. They hope they will stop being so afraid. They hope they will someday be ready for friends.

It looked like Suzie might be one of those monkeys. The rescue center staff tried to put her with other Olive baboons. This made her afraid. She sat in the corner with her back to the other monkeys. When they came close, she screeched and ran away. She even bared her teeth to scare them away. She wanted nothing to do with them.

Leaving Suzie alone was the only choice, at first. The caretakers tried to make her happy in other ways.

Suzie had spent years of her life in a dark basement cage. This had made her pale and sick. The caretakers decided that Suzie needed fresh air and sunshine.

"When spring arrived, we moved Suzie's cage outside," Eileen said. "Right away, she seemed to bask in the sunshine. Her face tanned. She started to look like the Olive baboon she was meant to be."

Things were starting to get better for Suzie. One day they hoped Suzie could have a friend.

Bob's situation was different. He wasn't afraid of any monkey at the center. For a time, Bob was housed with Mighty. She was a macaque (sounds like mah-KAK) monkey who had come from a rescue center on Long Island, New York.

Like Suzie, Mighty had diabetes and needed a friend. But Bob had so much energy. He drove Mighty a little bit crazy. Bob and Mighty were not a good match.

Next, the caregivers decided to try pairing Bob with Suzie. And guess what? They liked each other!

Bob was smaller than the other Olive baboons, so Suzie wasn't so afraid of him. She was quiet, and Bob seemed to understand that.

Bob was still a crazy little monkey.

How Kids Can Help: Send a Care Package

Like other rescue groups, the Primate Rescue Center accepts cash donations to care for the animals. The center also has a wish list of items it hopes will be donated. If you see something you'd like to send, you can ship it to:

Primate Rescue Center
2515 Bethel Road
Nicholasville, KY 40356

Here are items from their wish list:

- ✓ Shredded wheat cereal
- ✓ Raisins
- ✓ Trail mix
- ✓ Nuts in shells
- ✓ Peanut butter
- ✓ Honey
- ✓ Graham crackers
- ✓ Pretzels
- ✓ Unsweetened coconut flakes
- ✓ Wood chips (pine, not cedar)
- ✓ Heavy brown paper leaf/yard bags

He buzzed around Suzie like a tornado. But she seemed to like watching him. It was odd, but the match worked. Suzie had a friend. And Bob had a quiet new granny.

Since Bob and Caleb were both Vervet monkeys, they seemed like a good match, too. So, the caretakers brought Caleb to the cage with Bob and Suzie. Caleb was a little shy at first. But in no time, Caleb and Bob were wrestling like brothers.

"You can tell Caleb looks up to Bob," Eileen said. "Caleb watches Bob and tries to be like him."

When Bob jumps into the sandbox full of sawdust to find hidden toys and treats, Caleb watches closely. He studies his brave new friend. Soon, he is ready to try the sandbox, too. When Bob swings or jumps or scampers, Caleb is usually close behind.

All three monkeys are close, Eileen said. "Usually, when primates are not closely bonded, they will walk away when another one comes near them. Or they will turn their backs and ignore them. That does not happen in this group. Suzie will sit by and watch the boys. They run by her and wrestle around her."

So, Suzie, Bob, and Caleb became a happy family. They live together and enjoy each other's company. They have plenty of food to eat. They have good care and exercise. Most of all, they have each other.

THE END

DON'T MISS!

NATIONAL GEOGRAPHIC
KIDS **CHAPTERS**

CROCODILE ENCOUNTERS!

And More True Stories of Adventures With Animals

By Brady Barr With Kathleen Weidner Zoehfeld

NATIONAL GEOGRAPHIC

Turn the page for a sneak preview . . .

My team and I are ready for our dangerous mission in Tanzania.

Croc DISGUISE

Hi, my name is Brady Barr, and I'm a zoologist. That means I study animals. I've studied all kinds of animals in about 70 countries on Earth. But of all the animals I've worked with, crocodiles are my favorite.

There are 23 different types, or species, of crocodilians (sounds like krah-koh-DIL-ee-uhns). I've had the chance to see them all in the wild. I've been up close to the wide-snouted alligators and caimans (sounds like KAY-mens). I've been nose-to-nose with the narrow-jawed crocodiles. And I've even studied the weird and wonderful gharial (sounds like GAR-ree-uhl).

Sometimes I have to catch wild crocodiles for my work. For some studies, my team and I need to weigh and measure crocs. For other studies, we need to attach high-tech devices to the crocs. These devices help us keep track of the crocs, or they record information about changes in the areas where the crocs live.

The number of people on Earth is growing every year. More humans on the planet means people need more space. People are moving into areas that were once the wild homes, or habitats, of crocs. With their habitats shrinking, many species of crocodilians are dying out. When a species is dying out, we say it is an endangered species.

The more we know about endangered species and what they need, the better we can help them. But catching wild crocs is a dangerous job—for me and for the crocs!

To catch a croc, I usually have to snare it with a rope. Then I wrestle it until it is very tired. I jump onto its back and tie its jaws shut so it can't bite. Then I tie its legs. That's a lot easier said than done!

Even a tired crocodile is very strong. Catching one can turn dangerous quickly. Crocodiles are not used to having people jump on their backs. It is strange for them.

That's why I am always looking for better ways to handle the crocs and get the information we need.

We know that crocodiles are calmer around other crocs than around humans.

Did You Know?

Crocodiles have the strongest bite force on Earth. It's so strong, it's close to the bite force of a *Tyrannosaurus rex*.

If only another croc could find out what we need to know. Then it wouldn't be so hard on the animal we want to study.

Well, on a trip to Tanzania (sounds like Tan-zan-EE-uh), I got to find out what it feels like to be a croc.

It all started when I was giving a talk to a group of children at their school. I was telling them about my work with crocodiles. One small boy raised his hand.

"Dr. Brady," he asked, "why don't you dress up as a croc and join their club?"

At the time, I thought that was pretty funny. I laughed and went on with my talk. But I couldn't shake the idea from my mind. *Could it actually work?* I wondered. There was one way to find out!

I asked the people at National Geographic if they could build me a lifelike crocodile suit. Luckily, they were up for the job!

Artists made the head from a mold of a real crocodile head. That made it look exactly like the real thing! It was made of a material called polystyrene (sounds like pahl-ee-STYE-reen). It is very lightweight, but strong.

Next, the engineers built the body. This part was important. It needed to protect my body if an angry croc decided to bite!

They made a set of metal ribs. These formed a strong cage around me. Then the cage was covered by a shield made of Kevlar. The same stuff is used to make bulletproof vests. That would make it hard for even a croc bite to break through!

Finally, the artists made a rubber cape that looked just like crocodile skin. This would cover the body and make it look like a real croc.

At last, my croc suit was ready. And boy, did it look real! My plan was to get close enough to a group of wild crocs to put high-tech devices on their backs.

If my test was going to work, I would have to make the crocs believe I was one of them.

WANT TO KNOW WHAT HAPPENS NEXT?
Be sure to check out *Crocodile Encounters!*
Available wherever books and
ebooks are sold.

INDEX

Boldface indicates illustrations.